The Monster
UNDER THE BED

Written by Deb Eaton
Illustrated by Lina Chesak

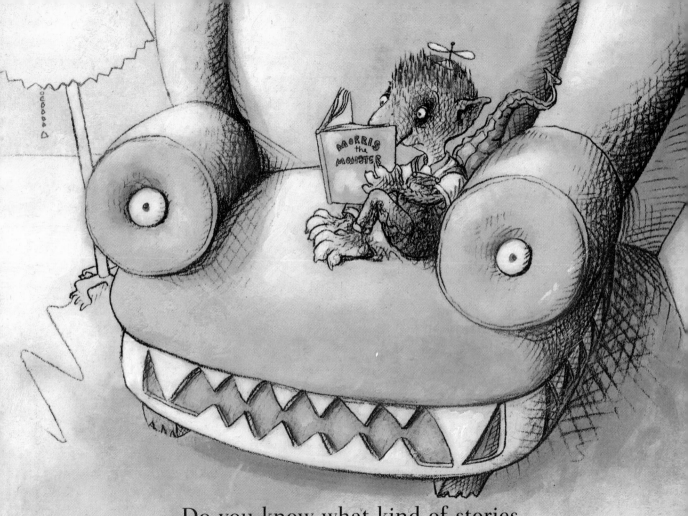

Do you know what kind of stories
monsters read? Monster stories!

Mama Monster was reading a story to
her beautiful monster children. "This is a
story about Morris the Monster," she said.
And this is what Mama Monster read . . .

4

Morris had beautiful red fur and beautiful
purple ears and a beautiful, large nose.

He lived in a beautiful, dark cave in a dark, dark woods.

6

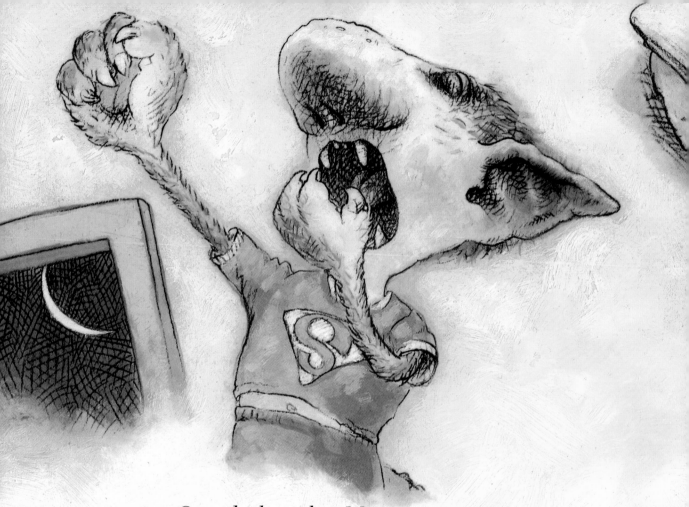

One dark night, Morris was getting
ready for bed. He put on his purple pjs.

He was just about to turn out the
light when . . .

Erf-erf-erf.

What was that?

Morris turned this way and that.
But he didn't see anything.

Erf-erf-erf.

There it was again.

Was it in the yard? Morris got up and
looked in the yard. But he didn't see anything.

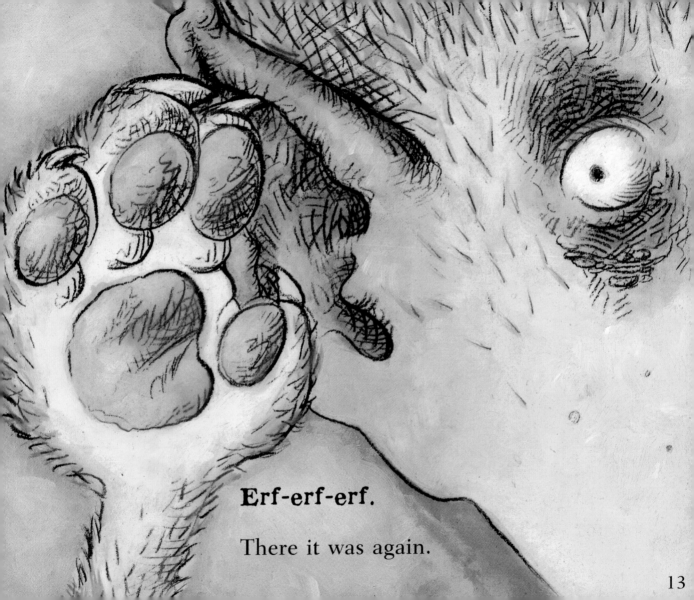

Erf-erf-erf.

There it was again.

Was it hiding in his large toy car?
Morris looked in his large toy car. But he
didn't find anything.

Erf-erf-erf.

There it was again.

Was it hiding under his purple shirt?
Morris looked under his purple shirt. But he
didn't find anything.

Well, monsters should not get upset about
a funny sound! Right? So Morris got into bed.

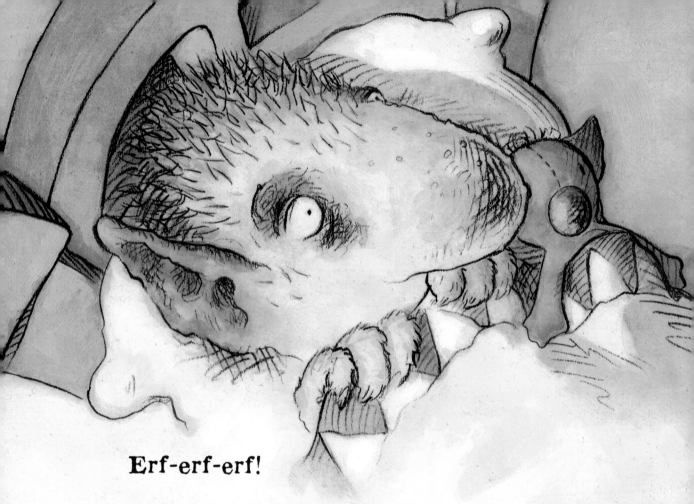

Erf-erf-erf!

Oh, no! There it was again. It was really loud this time!

And this time, Morris knew where to
look. It was coming from under the bed!

Morris knew he had to look. But it was
dark under there! Slowly, he poked his nose
under the bed.

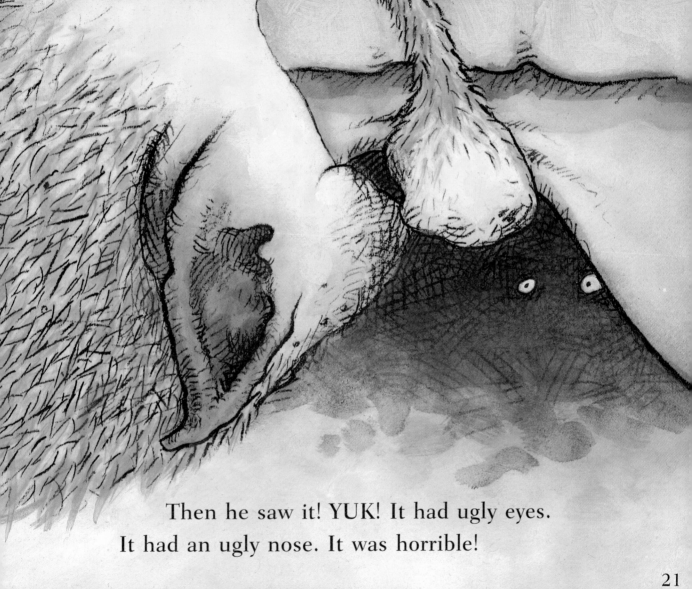

Then he saw it! YUK! It had ugly eyes.
It had an ugly nose. It was horrible!

21

Morris screamed a loud monster scream.

ARRRRG!

The puppy barked a loud puppy bark.

Erf-erf-erf!

Then the puppy ran out of the room. It ran far, far away.

"Oooo! That was a good story!" said
the beautiful monster children. "Read it
again, Mama! Read it again!"

9 2 3 8